9/02

W9-AGM-946

MIDLOTHIAN
PUBLIC LIBRARY

Bilingual Edition

READING POWER

Edición Bilingüe

Hulk Hogan

Wrestling Pro

Campeón de lucha libre

Heather Feldman

Traducción al español
Mauricio Velázquez de León

The Rosen Publishing Group's
PowerKids Press™ & **Buenas Letras**™
New York

1

For Sophie Megan
Para Sophie Megan

Published in 2002 by The Rosen Publishing Group, Inc.
29 East 21st Street, New York, NY 10010

First Bilingual Edition 2002
First Edition in English 2001

Book Design: Michael de Guzman

Photo Credits: pp. 5, 9, 11, 13, 15, 17, 21 © Colin Bowman; pp. 7, 19 © The Everett Collection.

Feldman, Heather.
    Hulk Hogan : wrestling pro = Hulk Hogan : campeón de lucha libre / Heather Feldman : traducción al español Mauricio Velázquez de León.
        p. cm.— (Reading power)
    Includes index.
    Summary: A brief biography of the professional wrestler, focusing on his exploits in the ring, his career as a movie actor, and his charity work.
    ISBN 0-8239-6140-0 (alk. paper)
    1. Hogan, Hulk, 1955—Juvenile literature. 2. Wrestlers—United States—Biography—Juvenile literature. [1. Hogan, Hulk, 1955– 2. Wrestlers. 3. Spanish language materials—Bilingual.] I. Title.
    II. Series.

GV1196.H64 F45 2001
796.812'092—dc21
[B]

Word Count:
English: 129
Spanish: 128

Manufactured in the United States of America

2

Contents

Contenido

Hulk Hogan is a great wrestler. Hulk Hogan is very strong.

———

Hulk Hogan es un gran luchador. Hulk Hogan es muy fuerte.

4

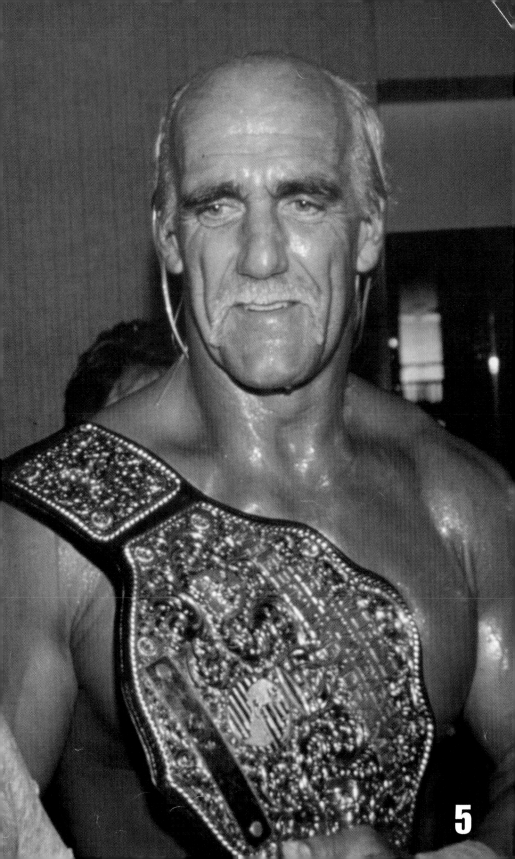

5

Hulk Hogan uses a weight machine. Hulk lifts weights to stay strong.

Hulk Hogan utiliza una máquina para levantar pesas. Así se conserva en buena forma.

Hulk Hogan shows off his big muscles.

———————

A Hulk Hogan le gusta mostrar sus músculos.

9

Hulk Hogan wrestles in a ring. Hulk Hogan has many fans. Lots of people like to watch him wrestle.

———

Hulk Hogan lucha en un cuadrilátero *(ring)*. Hulk Hogan tiene muchos seguidores. ¡Muchas personas disfrutan al verlo luchar!

Hulk Hogan wins a belt for wrestling. Hulk Hogan is a wrestling pro.

Hulk Hogan gana un cinturón de lucha. Es un campeón de lucha libre.

Hulk Hogan talks to a reporter. Reporters ask Hulk questions because he is famous. Hulk meets a lot of people.

Hulk Hogan habla con un reportero. Los reporteros le hacen preguntas porque él es famoso. Hulk conoce a muchas personas.

Hulk Hogan met
Muhammed Ali.

Hulk Hogan conoce
a Muhammed Ali.

Hulk Hogan was in the movie *Rocky III*. Hulk played a mean wrestler named Thunderlips.

Hulk Hogan salió en la película *Rocky III*. Hulk interpretó a un luchador malvado de nombre *Thunderlips*.

19

These children have bandannas like Hulk Hogan. These children like Hulk Hogan. Lots of people like Hulk Hogan!

Estos niños llevan pañuelos en la cabeza como los de Hulk Hogan. ¡A muchas personas les cae muy bien Hulk Hogan!

Glossary

bandanna (ban-DA-nah) Colorful cloth worn on the head.

belt (BEHLT) What a wrestler gets for winning a match.

fans (FANZ) People who like a famous person.

muscles (MUH-suhlz) Parts of the body underneath the skin that can be tightened or loosened to make the body move.

reporter (re-POR-ter) a person who tells people the news.

weights (WAYTS) Heavy objects that are lifted for exercise.

Glosario

cinturón (el) Lo que obtiene un luchador cuando gana una lucha.

músculos (los) Órganos del cuerpo que se encuentran debajo de la piel y que pueden contraerse o estirarse para producir movimiento.

pesas (las) Objetos pesados que se levantan para hacer ejercicio.

reportero Una persona que trabaja en periódicos, radio o televisión y realiza reportajes o da noticias.

seguidores (los) Personas que siguen o admiran la carrera de una persona famosa.

Here are more books to read about wrestling:

Para leer más acerca de la lucha libre, te recomendamos estos libros:
Wrestling Renegades: An In-Depth Look at Today's Superstars of Pro Wrestling
by Daniel Cohen. Archway (1999)

Superstars of Men's Pro Wrestling
by Matthew Hunter
Chelsea House Publishers (1998)

To learn more about Hulk Hogan, check out these Web sites:

Para aprender más sobre Hulk Hogan visita esta página de Internet:
http://www.wrestlingmuseum.com/pages/bios/hogan2.html
http://www.wcwwrestling.com/1999/superstars/hogan/

Index

Índice